I Still Have Nothing to Say … so I Write

POEMS AND THOUGHTS

KEN SKOBY

I STILL HAVE NOTHING TO SAY ... SO I WRITE POEMS AND THOUGHTS

Copyright © 2020 Ken Skoby.

All rights reserved. No part of this book may be used or reproduced by any means, graphic, electronic, or mechanical, including photocopying, recording, taping or by any information storage retrieval system without the written permission of the author except in the case of brief quotations embodied in critical articles and reviews.

iUniverse books may be ordered through booksellers or by contacting:

iUniverse
1663 Liberty Drive
Bloomington, IN 47403
www.iuniverse.com
1-800-Authors (1-800-288-4677)

Because of the dynamic nature of the Internet, any web addresses or links contained in this book may have changed since publication and may no longer be valid. The views expressed in this work are solely those of the author and do not necessarily reflect the views of the publisher, and the publisher hereby disclaims any responsibility for them.

Any people depicted in stock imagery provided by Getty Images are models, and such images are being used for illustrative purposes only. Certain stock imagery © Getty Images.

ISBN: 978-1-5320-9100-1 (sc)
ISBN: 978-1-5320-9101-8 (hc)
ISBN: 978-1-5320-9102-5 (e)

Library of Congress Control Number: 2019921233

Print information available on the last page.

iUniverse rev. date: 01/08/2020

DEDICATION

To my son:
Aaron Skoby

Nancy Tkachuk for her insights,
wisdom and artistic visions.

Mae B., Nicholas M. & Nicholas M Skoby Jr.

Sheryl D., Steve T. and Vic A.

Life can be a long, winding wonder filled
road with numerous crossroads.
Thank you to all those past and present
that have touched my life!

*There are moments in life
when connections are so compelling
that just one lifetime
cannot explain their intensity.*

CONTENTS

POEMS

The Walk	1
In A Time Gone By	2
The Wonderness Of Life	4
Gold	5
White	6
Lived	7
The Trip	8
Morning Rush	9
Seasons	10
Birches	11
The Struggle Within	12
Liberated	13
Skyline	14
Goldmine	15
Steps	16
Climb	17
The Lake	18
One	19
Wheelbarrow's Breeze	20
The Moon	22
Maine	23
Eye Of The Storm	24
The Coat	25
The Search	26
Growth	27
Hope	28
Holding Back Time	30
Thunder's Sight	31
C'est La Vie	32

Frost Flower	33
It's Okay	33
Like A Spring	34
Flown	35
Breath	36
Visions	37
No Regret	38
First Light	39
Stress	*40*
Seed In The Wind	41
Midnight Queen	42
Floating Free	43
Rainbows And Deer	44
Fireflies' Dance	45
Autumn Sky	46
Twilight	47
Autumn Life	48
Falinter Oak	49
The Canvas	50
Traces	51
Winter Sunset	52
Caressing Fog	53
Through A Window	54
Three Precious Gifts	55
Life	56
Silhouettes	57
The Stone	58
Rainbows End	59
Essence Of Friends	60
Spring	61
Where You Will Find You	62
Whispers In The Wind	64
Cashmere Clouds	65
Reflecting	66
Open Space	67

Fireworks 68
Slip Away 69
Outside Inside 70
Friends 71
Thin 72
Tears In The Dark 73
Slapped 74
Freedom 75
One Night's Window 76
Soul Touch 78
Later 78
Soul Warrior 79
Music 80
Eyes 81
Fiddlehead'en 82
Renegade 83
Pale Rider 84
July Lights 85
Innocent 86
Innocence 87
Perspectives 88
Vision Rising 90

FOUND POEMS

Lit 94
Cabaret 94
Innkeeper 95
Demons 95

INTERACTIVE POEM

Scramble 96
Create 98
Create 99

HAIKU'S

THOUGHTS

Time	137
Silence	143
Life	149
Fear	163
Teachers	165
Senses	181
Courage	182
Failure	183
Love	185
Winter	186
Paradise	187
The Mind	188
P	189
T	189
Imagine	190
Memories	192
The Touch	194
Why	195
The Marionettes	196
Create	197
Create	198
Create	199

JUST FOR FUN

Picture These	201
Thrill Of A Lifetime	206

POEMS

THE WALK

Step by step a wander through time,
wondering where I've been.
Walk with me…

I look… saturated with visions of life,
drifting within these eyes.
Look with me…

I listen… as nature's songs hum in rhyme,
dancing in the stratosphere.
Listen with me…

I touch… watching ripples in the water,
circling outward in stillness.
Touch with me…

I sense… aromas floating on a breeze,
smiles gliding on evergreens.
Sense with me…

I speak with nature as it crosses the wind,
hinting of hope for humanity.
Speak with them.

IN A TIME GONE BY

A walk through the woods,
where my grandfather stood.
Sounds from a brook, draw me in for a look.

Sun peeks through the rain,
flowers fragrances remain.
Fiddleheads are curled tight,
reaching for springs early light.
I took in every sound,
wildflowers abound.
In a time gone by.

Slippers of pink, yellow, white,
commanding a glorious sight.
Violets of white, yellow, blue,
velveteen covered with dew.
It is here that I grew,
in my point of view.
In a time gone by.

Across the forest floor,
inspirations did soar.
Darting insects flew,
trout leapt to the blue.
I relaxed in the sun,
as we all became one.
In a time gone by.

I had nothing to fear,
reflections were clear.
There is so much to revere,
in nature's vibrant frontier.
No matter the cost,
this cannot be lost.
Ghosts…
of a time gone by.

THE WONDERNESS OF LIFE

When to come, when to go, time goes by.
Live today, or try to grow, time will fly.
Don't worry of the little things,
a word, a view, the strife.
Focus on the best of it,
the elegance of life.

Don't worry of doctor bills,
or where the money went.
Don't stress about existence,
or what that person meant.
For you may never sense,
the sky, the land, or sea.
A mind caught by worry,
is a mind that is not free.

A tree stands tall in glory,
an enduring work of art.
Only on its grandest day,
its touch reaches a heart.
Minds are bent on other things,
a word, a view, the strife.
One will miss the greatest gift…
The wonderness of life.

GOLD

I met a man upon a road,
if any truth shall be told,
I thought he had no gold.

We climbed as we walked,
sharing lives as we talked.
No phones, TV or a clock,
as we paused upon a rock.

He had his stories of the day,
how he came to be this way.
As we set forth to depart,
he left me a last thought.

No fears nor tears for me,
life is simple… I am free.
Life is as it's meant to be,
I truly sense all you see.

I continued along that road,
one last truth must be told,
It was I… Who possessed no gold.

WHITE

Softly settled snow, paints a forest window,
bends a young birch, where cardinals perch.
Tracks of a doe with a yearling in tow,
are meandering quietly below.
Spruce is the scent, playing like an instrument.

I turn for a glance… Snow sprites chant.

A shimmering light, burst forth in delight,
by a bold flowing brook, I pause for a look.
Mourning doves sing, as they take wing,
a partridge shows flare, its senses aware.

I turn for a glance… Snow sprites prance.

Crystal daggers suspend in light,
revealing a kaleidoscope's sight.
Colors contrast, as time soars past,
nature stands tall, so let the snow fall.

Turn for a glance… Snow sprites dance.

LIVED

I've lived and died, screamed at the sky,
touched anguish and pain, cried in rain.
Sat with the pines, twisted with vines,
resting my head, on natures soft bed.
I travel in rhyme, searching for time,
laugh and sigh… Smile at the sky.
Sat in stillness on Earth,
while nature gave birth.
Tasted dawn's dew,
been lost… But still grew.
Shed most of my fears,
touched heavenly tears.
Made angels in the snow,
ran *fast*… But lived slow.
I fought tooth and claw,
for the miracles I saw,
here… In Shangri-La.

As I look back, there was nothing I lacked.
I would not change a thing… That's a fact!
I have lived.

THE TRIP

My dad and I jump in the car late at night,
to pick up my brother from his long flight.
We laugh and brag once his feet hit ground,
back to the car, there are fish to be found.
Talk and catch up, drive through the night,
headlights on camp, what a beautiful sight.
We unlock the door, pushing spiders away,
leave us alone, we won't care if you stay.
I switch on the light and start to unpack,
pause for a moment, it's good to be back.
Just an hour of sleep for heaven's sake,
but we are here… There is the lake!
Freeing my mind, wishing for light,
didn't take long, dreams took flight.
The water is calm, the loons cry,
the sky is blue, as the eagles fly.
I watch the show to feed their tribe,
waiting… To realize our fishing vibe.

MORNING RUSH

A whistle from a teapot,
feet hit the floor in a shot.
Scent of bacon in the air,
fly right by, I don't care.
Out the door to the lake,
no time now, for a break.
Grab my pole, hit the dock,
cast it to my favorite rock.
Smiling widely as I throw,
caught a fish, watch it grow…
They won't know.
The lake's alive with signs of fish,
breakfast is over, that is my wish.
We grasp the rods and a raincoat;
the time has come… To the boat!
In lake's reflection we begin to cast,
sharing the memories from our past.
It's not about fish, it's about the soul,
the smiles in time from a fishing pole.

SEASONS

Winds whistle softly, dancing through the trees,
ice grasps tightly as it tangos a gentle breeze,
I trot briskly... Waltzing the winter's freeze.

Scents of Spring, so much to be seen,
eyes walk about and then in between,
seeking first glimpses of early green.

Hummingbirds frozen, still in midflight,
fireflies igniting, the fields in the night,
marshmallows roasting, in soft firelight.

Autumns bursting with echoes of hues,
thundering wings of geese as they flew,
embedding in minds like natures tattoo.

BIRCHES

There is splendor in these trees,
watch them yield to the breeze.
In every line and curl of bark,
time touches and left its mark.
Nature's laws are very clear,
winters marked another year.

Trees splinter from winds and snow,
life takes some, while others grow.
It bows humble with every branch,
reaching for life at every chance.
Simple reflections to awaken sight,
for this is Life, in black and white.

THE STRUGGLE WITHIN

Walk inward, with the wind to your back,
what surrounds you is now turning black.
Blind eyes, deaf ears, wandering the dark,
a mind must receive to reach for a spark.
Surrounded by keys, but can't find a lock,
eyes and ears floating, watching the clock.
 Searching for light inside the soul,
 living a life in search of your role.
  So, pause for a look,
  live your own book.
   Continue.

LIBERATED

My course altered
the moment I realized
that I had been missing.
I was a prisoner in time,
caught in an ever-turning cycle,
surrounded by my own makings.
I needed to breathe, slow and deep,
I needed to open my eyes...
Not just to see, but to perceive past them.
I needed to listen... Not to hear,
but, to sense what had surpassed me.
I needed to touch... Not for contact,
but to reach what was beyond.
I needed the innocent wisdom of nature.
I Breathe... Smell... Listen... Touch...See...
Now I taste it... The essence of freedom.

SKYLINE

The artificial light,
rips away the night,
killing innocent sight.

Tar, steel and concrete,
from buildings to street,
steals *caress* from one's feet.

Cultures wedded to phones,
echo blind stirring bones…
With the strangest of tones.

Skylines with tears,
impenetrable airs…
Lost empty stares.

Fields of feet talking,
sleepers are walking…
Wonder is stopping.

GOLDMINE

Wealth won or lost, is just a game,
success or failure, it's all the same.
Tiger or butterfly, one can choose,
the maze is there, filled with clues.

Fragile petals or unyielding trees,
broken branches or float a breeze.
Rushing past a flower's life,
to satisfy some inner strife.
Celebrate the flower's gift,
sense it's life... Visions drift.

Understand the earth's glow,
fly above... Then float low.
It matters not where you roam,
you shall find a new way home.
So, which way are you inclined,
what exactly is your goldmine?

STEPS

A first step, the bond of trust,
overwhelmed but seek we must.
Testing cold waters cautiously,
traversing ideas, starting to see.
I disagree but respect your stand,
we were not dealt a matching hand.
Each in life carry messages to learn,
as answers appear within every turn.
We shall find some common ground,
for that is how true friends are found.
Silent walk into the sky,
step up where eagles fly.
Reach beyond a single concept,
wonder where all secrets slept.
Talk as one, as you travel time,
focus upon each other's climb.
Keep walking that extra mile,
uncovering that elusive smile.
Walk into a magnificent day,
grinning having this to say...
Friend.

CLIMB

Walk through windows,
embedded in your brain.
Walk the empty highways,
while waltzing in the rain.
Reach a higher mountain,
to where you never climb.
Sweep away the cobwebs,
deposited there by time.

Swim the hostile waters,
filled with gold and tin.
Shattering the cubicle,
one called life within.
Ignore the fools fighting,
for what they help along.
Inwardly ever knowing,
what you see is wrong.

Always look forward,
climbing to the dawn.
Ascending oblivion...
Living life head-on.

THE LAKE

Water scurries to the shore,
always leads me to its door.
The softest hint, a silent hush,
waiting for a souls first rush.

Watching for the quiet loon,
it will be calling very soon.
Listen for its lingering tune,
haunting songs sung in June.

I digress to memory rock,
waiting for the fish to talk.
Two eagles are flying high,
just above from where I lie.

Tranquility surrounds a lake,
calming souls for life's sake.
Water scurries to the shore,
always leads me to its door.

ONE

Water murmurs within the trees,
gently touching the soft breeze.
Jack and Jill's and trillium,
do not judge why I've come.

It's all here for one to see,
I am them; they are me.
As I wander in the dream,
we are one, we are a team.

Listen, to a whip-poor-will,
close your eyes and be still.
If you are king or butterfly,
we would live the same sky.

It's all here for one to see,
we are them; they are we.
Living softly is the key,
leaving it for all to see.

Be humbled within the wood,
this is where our fathers stood.

WHEELBARROW'S BREEZE

Summer's here, let's find the tribe,
now is the time to explore outside.
Hide and seek is the game today,
time to hide… Now on your way.
Quiet laughter from shadow trees,
seeking them should be a breeze.

As we count with sweeping eyes,
I spied it there… Upon that rise.
Others took their turn to hide,
we meandered to take a ride.
Fell right out, got back in,
laughing at my grassy shin.

Now it's time to go and look,
just five minutes was all it took.
My turn to hide, so off I go,
no laughing… Go very slow.
Walking lightly as the deer,
that will help me disappear.

I shall hide under an evergreen tree,
they'll walk right by and never see.
I never spoke or made a sound,
that is why I was never found.
I sauntered out the final one,
"not fair", they said, "you've always won."

Discouraged faces all around,
I pointed out what I had found.
"We'll take turns," I said with pride,
"let's all go for a wheelbarrow ride."
Jump right in, do not be afraid,
we shall rest later in the shade.

This old wheelbarrow saved the day,
as we spent hours in our field ballet.
If you could have seen the laughing eyes,
the childish wonder… Their surprise.
You'd think we traveled across great seas,
but no…
Just the magic of a wheelbarrow's breeze.

THE MOON

My grandmother said,
while tucking me into bed,
Someday... We will go to the moon!

She sat by the window every night,
gazing at its shimmering light.
I still hear her radio play,
as she slowly drifted away.

She stared toward the light,
with her wish in plain sight.
She believed in the dream,
soaring on her moonbeam.

She passed away,
before I could say,
"You left us too soon.
we went to the moon."

She didn't care,
she was already there.

MAINE

Inspiration's flow is here then there,
bees, plants and trees and in the air.
Insects, mammals or birds in flight,
often cryptic, always in plain sight.
Rivers, lakes and the mighty sea,
nature's inspirations flowing free.
One word, song or a joyful tear,
a smile, touch, or sound I hear.
The sun, moon, and clouds with rain,
cherished thoughts bring me to Maine.

It is not the thought that inspires,
it is the pure simplicity of the spark.

EYE OF THE STORM

There's a storm in this heart,
at times, it has split me apart.
Centering now, the sky is blue,
but, I'm only half way through.
Time is stirring, it shall not wait,
words are my lines that illustrate.

Expectations led me to reach high,
tempests clearing, so into the sky.
I leapt head long, into the storm,
wore no coats, to keep me warm.
All memories still awake inside,
life is still a wonder filled ride.

Fly head-on into the soul of storms.
Touching life… As it all transforms.

THE COAT

Woven with happy memories,
sewn with fine embroideries,
I made myself a coat,
wore it heel to throat.

Soon imposters made their way,
claimed they tailored it that day.
I let it go to watch their game,
for it could never be the same.

Oh life…Just let it be,
it is just a coat,
it is not me.

THE SEARCH

There is nothing left to be said,
need a walk to clear my head.
Wisdom reveals the mighty sea,
senses abound, to set one free.

Feet wandering to a serene bay,
watching the bird's aerial ballet.
Sensing tides pulling out and in,
as the salty air touches my skin.

Jellyfish float as an angel's wing,
breakers hit rocks and sirens sing.
Hungry eyes, listening for a word,
lying suspended, visions blurred.

Cream foamed surf breaks to a roar,
floating seaweed searches for shore.
Periwinkles grasp the rocks so tight,
as life explodes in continuous flight.

A mind exposed, smelling every sound,
a quest is over…I have been found.

GROWTH

A lonely life on a single leaf,
wrapped inside a silky sheath.
A transformation very soon,
breaking free of its cocoon.

Your world now is the sky,
spread your wings and fly,
now's the time for you to try.

HOPE

Hope is wild, hope is free,
hope is all you want it to be.

If hope was a color,
it would overwhelm sight,
every hue, tint, or fusion,
would stimulate light.

Hope's are wishes,
dreams taking flight,
with echoes of rain,
and crickets at night.

Hope's sense will always remain,
singing softly, of loss and gain.
Extracts from life,
burst in on a breeze,
with essence of soil,
and evergreen trees.

Hope's touch will be soft and warm,
as sitting fireside, in a winter storm.
Gentle and soft as morning dew,
wondrous smiles beckon to you.

Hope's aromas, slip from the sky,
savory essences go streaming by.
Quiet hints arrive with the night,
musical dreams now take flight.

Hope is a wish, I cannot wish for you,
it comes from one's heart for it to be true.
Hope is desperate…What will you do?
Help find its way back…Through you.

HOLDING BACK TIME

Chasing dragons with a fishing net,
quietly stalking to catch you a pet.
Seeking a dream, we share a duet,
the fondest times you never forget.

To the lake we fish in search of gold,
your first fish you could hardly hold.
Jumping and laughing filled with glee,
all that we did, you were so carefree.

Closing my eyes can buy back time,
seconds past… Hear the clock chime.
Oh, there it is, that defining first sign,
he's on his way, he is no longer mine.

Loving and living will never hold back time,
so, I embrace memories that I can call mine.

THUNDER'S SIGHT

Gilded illuminations split through night,
penetrate black then burst intense white.
Silhouette shadows flash, fade and ignite,
overwhelming eyes with a fleeting sight.

Sequin coated windows burst and disappear,
as static rhythms transport music to the ear.
Gazing at darkness through the stratosphere,
abrupt severed light creates a new frontier.

Impulsive shimmers set fire to the sky,
winds caress trees, leaves learn to fly.
Visions form and strobe into the eyes,
nature explodes life, the sky complies.

C'EST LA VIE

Success or failure is all the same,
live life lost or hunger for gain.
Reach for a star, or walk in rain,
floating free or dragging a chain.

All one gains can be blown into dust,
glittering objects shall eventually rust.
Life may be ironic, so learn to adjust,
it may come down to a matter of trust.

Simple existence should not be in vain,
travel through life so not to cause pain.
Celebrate life with songs you sang,
balance it all with a yin and a yang.

Say *La Vie*,
let it be.
Such is life.

FROST FLOWER

Simple beauty from this crystal flora,
hues surging in the sunlight's aurora.
Mystical sights inside the crystalline,
every twinkling is a changing scene.
Morning's sun will end its reign,
lost flower on my window pane.

IT'S OKAY

Misunderstanding and misunderstood,
you cannot change it, if they would.
Do not cry, they will not sympathize,
do not help nourish their minds lie.
Free yourself, by letting it go,
many will just never know.
It's okay!

LIKE A SPRING

Life bursts forth like a spring,
wondering what life will bring.
Seeping past the toil and mud,
pulsing veins of epochs blood.

Aura's ignite of amber gold,
life hums songs a story told.
Seeking for a soul to sing,
waiting for a heart to ring.

Will we suffer or just weep,
struggle on or drift to sleep?
A gentle meander, to the keep,
a soothing nudge, into the deep.

Death bursts forth like a spring,
releases one soul, so it can sing.
Reaching unbound taking wing,
life bursts forth like the spring.

FLOWN

Standing alone on a beach,
horizon just out of reach,
so little here left to teach.

Existence that one must own,
pain assaults the brittle bone,
gazing at life and seeds sown.

Dreams rush in without relief,
remaining longer, in disbelief,
trying to shed a human sheath.

Voices beckon far from home,
reaching out into the unknown,
no longer one soars alone…
F
  l
    o
      w
        n

BREATH

Born with a deep quiet breath...

Soft tired soul struggling in the dark,
one more puzzle before it can depart.
Transcending portals in deepest night,
murmurs from souls, just out of sight.
Beyond dreams it's beginning to soar,
finding an answer, searching no more.

Lying awake but cannot flee the dead,
floating freely by a frayed silver thread.
Sensing freedom from deep underneath,
breaking its bonds from a human sheath.
Severing the thread, life is not in vain,
as an old soul soars without any pain.

Passing with a deep quiet breath...

VISIONS

Sitting and waiting for a petal to fall,
such a beautiful flower as it grew tall.
Life diversions are now out of reach,
Now no regretting, nothing to teach.
Winter is coming, winter is near,
one ends, one begins, so clear.
Death points to the tree of life,
ascending softly, releasing strife.

NO REGRET

He slowly gropes for his cigarettes,
as winds sway in a field of regrets.
Head down saunter, feeling the heat,
a musical wandering follows his feet.

Rain promenades where memories stood,
inwardly knowing he did what he could.
The regrets fond memories frozen in time,
two matching souls is a wonderful climb.

Somewhere hidden in a point of view,
every moment in life is why he grew.
Slowly groping for a cigarette,
realizing now… There is no regret.

FIRST LIGHT

As a curtain binding the light,
the blanket falls to signal night.
Buoyant shadows across the fields,
twilight darkens and the sun yields.

Gazing the sky as stars are born,
connecting dots as diagrams form.
Eyes breath await a shooting star,
sharper glimmers ignite from afar.

Opening eyes gaze to fields below,
seeking twinkles from high and low.
Sparks flickering are floating on air,
first here, there, then… Everywhere!

Sunrise is not the first dazzling light,
for one who seeks the edges of night.

STRESS

*My heads never clear,
been such a bad year,
seems nothing is near.
What am I doing here?*

It's such a lovely day,
I must pick a bouquet,
drink some Beaujolais
and let my mind play.

*I am filled with dread,
want to bang my head,
holding on by a thread,
should go back to bed.*

I shall drive to a bay,
treat it like a holiday,
may even see a ballet,
stop and eat at a café.

SEED IN THE WIND

Floating free on a breeze,
surveying all that it sees.
Pirouetting into the air,
sailing, without a care.

Searching for a quiet home,
a small piece of soft loam.
Nesting on perfect ground,
birth shall surely be found.

It does stand tall,
a part of the all,
bursting fences,
awakening senses.

Reborn...
More than just a seed in the wind.

MIDNIGHT QUEEN

The midnight Queen,
made the scene,
just to see the King.
Lights went down,
there was not a sound,
he began to sing.

In the heat of the lights,
he thought of the nights,
he was all alone…
His open heart, just a part,
of a body picked to the bone.

As he stared up to the moon,
he sang another tearful tune,
you don't know how lonely this can be.

The stage goes bare, but no one cares.
the show must go on.

FLOATING FREE

Amir's Song

Deep within these walls of stone,
can't you see you're not alone.
Life has frayed you to the bone,
searching for a new way home.
Let music ease the tone.

You could never find me,
there I was, floating free.
Gazing out beyond the sea,
searching for a magic key.
Let music help us see.

Each space holding memories,
Christmas lights upon the trees,
chimpanzees and chickadees,
marvelous starlight jamborees.
Let music release fantasies.

Now, here we are… Floating free.

RAINBOWS AND DEER

*Rainbows and deer magically appear,
and just as quickly disappear.*

In the first light of dawn,
does bring out their fawn.
Racing into an open field,
adults survey, fawns yield.
Youth exploring into a run,
bursting out under the sun.
Wary noses catch a breeze,
evaporating into the trees.
Vanished…

Dark clouds then thundering rain,
wind drives the sun, nature's gain.
In the expanse, explosions of blue,
bursting glimmers emitting a hue.
Rain and sun merge for the show,
rivals touch… A brilliant rainbow!
Stare in wonder, a childlike smile,
reflecting soft colors… So fragile.
Vanished…

FIREFLIES' DANCE

*Come one, come all
to the firefly's ball.*

All you need are nets and jars,
a little moonlight and the stars.
A childish heart to help you see,
entertainment shall set you free.

Foxtrot the moon to the hillside,
watch for lights, dreams collide.
Pirouetting nets, fireflies dance,
there is always a second chance.

Swing the nets, now into the jars,
as they all fill with the tiny stars.
Burst with laughter at the sight,
waltz together by firefly's light.

Now you know the fireflies dance,
I hope you frolic at every chance.

AUTUMN SKY

Orange moon sky
fills eyes with sound.
Fires burn clouds,
speak of colors found.

Silence in stillness,
echoes in ones' ear.
A breeze gliding by,
hums autumn's here.

An envelope opening,
light tears a new view.
Moon paints a picture,
each stroke a new blue.

Aura clouds wander,
as I bid my adieu.
Sleep eyes awaken,
spirit dreams flew.

TWILIGHT

The wind is calm,
the grass is still,
night has not yet fallen.

The moon lingers,
the light is hushed,
scratching echoes in the air.

New domains awaken,
clouds mute the pale,
reflections bursting pastels.

Crickets cheerful vocals,
conceal dropping light,
evening effortlessly emerges.

Shadows slowly lifting,
dreams begin to sing,
starlight shocks a silent sky.

Nature touches time,
fireflies appear...
Meadows magically ignite...Twilight.

AUTUMN LIFE

An exaggerated wind, sends chills in the air,
colorful soaring leaves, try to show their flair.
Meadows evolved amber, as they reminisce,
kaleidoscopes of color, with a blustery kiss.
Blushing trees turning, in a glorious style,
nature reaching life, shining in her smile.

Shadowed lights, reveal a stealthy forest maze,
sunlight peeks through, a thickened foggy haze.
Fresh worlds awaken, with life under the trees,
autumns' time stretching, inspecting all it sees.
A cold frenzied wind, stabbing like a knife,
as dry rustling leaves, teach the story of life.

Tree's paint exploding, exciting every sense,
constantly changing colors, is latent evidence.
A meandering of winds, are levitating leaves,
just a final glance, before the winter's freeze.
Breath becoming clouds, with a frosty stare,
autumn greeting winter, such a lovely pair.

FALINTER OAK

Harsh winds blowing...
Stripped naked but for a few memories
clinging to sight of its former splendor.

Icey brittle fingers depart...
Grasping tightly to the last of its coats,
falling snow, dress it magnificently.

Enduring strong and tall...
Glistening kisses of sun dance freely
illuminating life clinging to its' bones.

Hear the colors call...
Fluttering from its sheltering arms
defending life in its new horizon.

Snow falling silent...
Expose skeletons holding life,
dormant existence, living from within.

THE CANVAS

Darkness rolling in anger,
winds exclaim distress,
rain rapidly rigid.

Silence screams in anguish,
sight fleetingly blind,
visions veering violet.

Glimmers igniting canvas,
the color pallet grows,
shading soft scarlets.

Time is floating freely,
while waiting a reveal…
Perfectly painted portrait!

TRACES

Sounds of babbling waters,
while walking wonderland.
Catching childish laughter,
leaving traces in the sand.

Flowers igniting visions,
caress beauty in a dream.
Splashes touching silence,
leaving clouds in a stream.

Echoes becoming heavy,
winds share an icy stare.
Colors exploding boldly,
leaving music in the air.

Seasons slipping slowly,
frolicking in their glow.
Walking inside paradise,
left shadows in snow.

WINTER SUNSET

Dissipating sunlight,
birds soon disappear.
Sunset touches tree tops,
painting a crimson blush.

Whispers caress the snow,
winds beginning to slow.

Stillness grasps this moment,
as the masterpiece explodes.
Skies start dripping colors,
as clouds caress the light.

Wonder in this moment,
as nature gives consent.

Every stroke an accent,
light yields its descent.
Colors melting softly, touching every shore,
visions hugging gently, eyes stretch to soar.

CARESSING FOG

Soft walk inside the mist,
as moisture caresses skin.
Feet are speaking softly,
considering every stride.

Every scent is dripping,
stillness talks in the fog.
Traffic in the shadows,
a heart becomes alive.

Silence grabs the forest,
minds define the sound.
Imagination shimmers,
illusions graze the sky.

Marvels are a step away,
so, venture in their glow.
Take the time to wander,
watching wonders flow.

Become a rainbow in the fog.

THROUGH A WINDOW

Fields filled with wonder,
so softly appears the doe.
Movements in the pasture,
fawns wander to a window.

A child watches wonder,
all time has blown away.
Spirits caress a stillness,
new hearts begin to play.

Stop and stare in silence,
share each other's strife.
Each of us not knowing,
we shared…and saved a life.

THREE PRECIOUS GIFTS

Dedicated to Ramsey and Rascal

Three tiny balls, crying and cold,
not much more than two days old.
We bottle fed them into the night,
one had to let go; it lost its fight.

Two flourished, became part of our soul,
loving all eight of the hearts they stole.
We'd run home, awaiting their embrace,
first the hug, then they washed our face.

Affections they showed knew no bounds,
a nobler family, could not be found.
The wild called, so they soon went away,
one returned, we will not forget that day.

A year or two had quickly slipped by,
yet, there she was, stopping, to say hi.
There in the wood line, walking the wall,
a mother with babies, imagine, three in all!

A raccoon's love will always stay,
our little bandits of white, black and grey.

LIFE

Scintillating shards,
reach relentlessly.
Tormenting tragedies,
panicking past pain.

Deep, dark depressions,
woefully weeping.
Fractured fragments,
fluidly flow floating.

Happiness hoping,
tiredly trying.
Slumbering souls,
silently soaring.

Soft…
Still…

SILHOUETTES

We are ghosts' in time,
shadows of what has been.
Varying colors on an edge,
outlines artlessly misread.

Shapes that are distorted,
enhanced lines ill-sorted.
Profiles with no substance,
appearances bent by light.

Evolving and projecting,
slanted shadows glow.
Spirits slide suspended,
trace paths just below.

We are but silhouettes,
shadows left in time.
Ghosts in memories,
of what we leave behind.

THE STONE

A stone is thrown, what will you do?

Pick it up and throw it back,
it was an unprovoked attack.
Just wander to another track,
fear added to what you lack.

Freeze and feel total shock,
stop and consent it to block.
Step around the lonely rock,
leave it for another's walk.

Maybe ask what it meant,
it may be just an accident.
After all it makes no sense,
no need here to be so tense.

Pause when a rock is thrown,
consider we do not live alone.
Feel the journey of the stone,
it travels beyond just a poem.

RAINBOWS END

I refuse to come in from the rain,
the mind is clearer in its domain.
I refuse to walk with marionettes,
they use each word like bayonets.

Bitter speech has become too bold,
shadows stabbing as souls are sold.
Fearing ghosts, melting in the dark,
shooting fire yet, missing the mark.

Saw the clouds, yet still stood in the rain,
touched the gold, but didn't need its pain.
Smelled the smoke, departed the fire,
sensed the wall, leapt the barbwire.

Saw the crying, lying, and the strife,
yet still... Sought the rainbows in life.

ESSENCE OF FRIENDS

Friends are the joyful fawns in a field,
frolicking on an early spring morning.
The relaxed notes of mourning doves,
sending tender music floating the air.

Friends are the colorful feathered birds,
singing their melodies into memories.
Flowers dancing on a summer breeze,
on the clearest of the deep blue skies.

Friends are shades of a warm evening
with sun's ricocheting echoes of color.
The brushed vibrant hues on a canvas
that blissfully stroke the autumn trees.

Friends are the magnificent cardinals,
vividly accented in a new fallen snow.
The smiles of the friendly chickadees,
that caress the warmest spring breeze.

Friends never leave.

SPRING

Tye-dyed colors dripping, dry in the sky,
fluffy clouds smiling, just drifting high.
Tree life awakens, reaching for the sun,
fawns are frolicking, not to be outdone.

Colors begin expanding, flying in the fields,
winds begin to whisper, nature never yields.
Rains practice rhythms, in the morning dew,
nature starts singing, as doves begin to coo.

Flowers are caressing, just to kiss the rain,
petals begin bursting, soft notes in a refrain.
Chickadees are singing, eyes begin to drift,
nature is surrounding us, such a lovely gift.

Magnificent journeys, turning into smiles,
life is emerging, as visions float for miles.
Nature's views, show what a life is worth,
it's not about dying, it's all about rebirth.

WHERE YOU WILL FIND YOU

When a heart can no longer hold, eyes can no longer perceive, and a restless soul searches. These are places I found me.

Wandering into the twilights glow,
lingering intently for every show.
Skipping smooth rocks in the rain,
viewing the circles as they remain.

Walking a train track upon its rail,
sauntering beyond a wildlife trail.
Flushing partridge or even a doe,
awakening life, by taking it slow.

Viewing mists, upon an ocean shore,
senses exploding, eyes wanting more.
Mining seashells from a sandy grave,
dodging the wrath of an ocean wave.

Drifting delight, in a fresh winter snow,
skiing shadows, as winds begin to blow.
Birds rising off, the snow cloaked trees,
delivering songs, in their winter freeze.

Searching meadows, in morning dew,
watching eagles, enjoying their view.
Rainbow glitters, in the spider's web,
matted grass, where deer found a bed.

Smiles abound, beside every stream,
time explodes, colors ignite a dream.
Trout swimming by, leap for the sky,
then wait beneath, for one more try.

All steps accepted, adventure awaits,
nature's creations, boldly illustrates.
Eagles, hummingbirds or the moose,
tiger lily, lady slippers or the spruce.

A voyage is waiting, for a new view,
sharing in nature, you will find you.

WHISPERS IN THE WIND

I smell whispers in the wind.

Lilac, apple blossoms, evergreen,
hints of flora that cannot be seen.
Soft fragrances of the spring rain,
scents fly by, their songs remain.

I hear whispers in the wind.

The lakes, rivers, an ocean shore,
grasping for life, reaching its core.
Defining sounds before they pass,
touching their spirit, while it lasts.

I feel whispers in the wind.

Teachers appear within a breeze,
lessons wander through the trees.
Senses stream in, I begin to smile,
they caress the wisdom of a child.

I see the whispers in the wind.
I breathe the whispers in the wind.

CASHMERE CLOUDS

Cashmere clouds carry, a marshmallow dream,
fluorescence floating fog, sleeps above a stream.
Shimmery sun's shadows, dancing in the trees,
soft spoken snapdragons, allowing honey bees.

Cheeky chanting chickadees, erupting in song,
reflecting running robins, stop and sing along.
Happy hovering hummingbirds, float in midair,
elusive eager eagles, soaring by without a care.

Cashmere clouds censor, softened tender light,
flying floating fairies, gliding on minds sight.
Hurrying halfling hobbits, running in the glen,
fantastic fantasy flowers, every now and then.

Marvel at your visions, every chance you can,
touch a daydream now... If not, then when?

REFLECTING

It is perplexing to me, how a life bends,
pondering the moments, each song ends.
Feet touch softly, as a mind tries to soar,
touching a smile, shall leave a new door.

A thoughtful amble, reaching the mind,
memories of what, was not left behind.
Sketches in moments, turn in the brain,
portraits in puddles, are seen in the rain.

Traces upon a wind, provide a window,
surveying memories, feeling their flow.
Every step forward, shape us like clay,
a gentle reminder, now's the new day.

Simple reflection, shall help set one free,
making life's scars, just marks on a tree.
Traversing a life, could become intense,
sooner or later… It makes perfect sense.

OPEN SPACE

Walk with the wind, as it touches your face,
let beliefs wander, while touching its grace.
Moments in time, will float through the air,
thoughts paint pictures, remembering there.

Talk with the snow, as you stand in its field,
discover the moments, that one must yield.
Nature shall lead you, a multitude of ways,
some enter easily, others touching delays.

Listen to a river flow, as it sings its song,
touching all its life, of a journey so long.
Sense all the living, its veins will provide,
access its rhythms, let nature be the guide.

Stand on a mountain, surveying its view,
fly with the eagles, breathing the blue.
Reach for a rainbow, walk to its gate,
share your travels, it's never too late.

Please, remember…Life is not a race.
Walk with style…To that open space.

FIREWORKS

In the expanse an explosion of blues,
red, yellow, green every virtual hue.
Skies blending colors, into the night,
dripping in gold, blushing the white.

Jaw open sights, touching the shine,
chills running up and down the spine.
Outlines are burning, wandering wild,
Reminiscing, with the eyes of a child.

Colors are exploding, like broken glass,
aromas now smolder, as they float pass.
Thundering flashes, as the colors spray,
blasting the light, as dark turns to gray.

Sounds of slapping, as mosquitos appear,
youngsters scurrying, trying to disappear.
Heading for home, as tired eyes stray,
all in all…It was a wonder filled day.

SLIP AWAY

Somehow, somewhere it slipped away,
rolling like thunder, in a floating ballet.
Harvesting fragments, yearning to stay,
memory mountains, stand in your way.

With each step, something new is born,
emotions in pieces, still feeling forlorn.
Sense vibrant roses, but feeling a thorn,
needing to speak, yet still you are torn.

Awaken life, when one stands alone,
wherever you are, becomes a home.
Building begins, with a single stone,
healing follows, every broken bone.

Time will always slip away,
now is always the new day.
Try to be your own bouquet,
reach to find your own way.

Then silently...
Just slip away.

OUTSIDE INSIDE

Lost and lonely yet never alone,
floating adrift reaching for home.
Surrounded, powerfully confused,
upset, shattered then feeling used.

Wandered in darkness, as it came for a kill,
when a quiet light shown, a way to be still.
Senses wide open, as miracles appeared,
dark clouds scatter, as new lessons neared.

Harmony surrounds us, unwind for a look,
contemplate moments, breathe by a brook.
Life will vanish, when chasing the moon,
as a song disappears, deprived of its tune.

Music surrounds us, it waits to be heard,
the gentlest crescendos, from every bird.
Trees strip bare, in a cold winter's freeze,
life will return, on a warm spring breeze.

Fog will scatter, as a soul becomes bright,
when the child awakens, seeing the light.

FRIENDS

Thank you for the patience with me,
if not for you I would be lost at sea.
Life, love, laughs, in the open space,
family, friends, faith, touching grace.

I need no proof, to believe in you all.
When time was tough, you stood tall.
I sensed you all, as you trusted in me,
together strong, as it was meant to be.

    We are all but waves in time.
          Thank you…
    For being part of my climb.

THIN

Burning so hot,
ashes blow out the door.
Not far behind,
gone searching for more.

Eyes look around,
nothing touching skin.
A wandering life,
spread a hair too thin.

Every step,
just charms on a chain.
Every contact,
leaves colors that stain.

This becomes a life,
standing idle in rain.
Drops touching skin as,
they attempt to explain.

Trust in your heart, trust in your soul.
Life cannot be in your control.

TEARS IN THE DARK

Sitting alone with tears in the dark,
moments in life leaving their mark.
Nocturnal silence views a soul soar,
watchers are fighting a lonely war.

Sitting alone with tears in the dark,
naked spirit's flow starting a spark.
Passionate songs reaching the soul,
joy bursting out smolders like coal.

Sitting alone with tears in the dark,
flashes of senses reaching the heart.
When ones alone needing a smile,
walk the path of their lonely trial.

Sitting alone with tears in the dark,
paint in all colors becomes the art.
If you stain a life, try to save two,
time will not heal all one can do.

Sitting alone with smiles in the dark…

SLAPPED

Standing transparent in the rain,
sorrow running through a brain.
Restless stirrings inside a head,
pondering that which lies dead.

A walk in the woods, searching a ridge,
perceiving a river, but seeking a bridge.
Swollen and reckless, the streams flow,
searching for light, to bathe in its glow.

Souls ache when slapped by greed,
cuts run deep yet you cannot bleed.
The mind races with infinite speed,
allow what is, to be standing freed.

Let the winds shift where they may,
as all life lessons, mold us like clay.
Falling angels, struggle here on earth,
wandering and waiting for a rebirth.

All of life is meant to be beautiful,
sense one's heart, for its true miracle.

FREEDOM

Silently watching one more sacrifice,
words thrown without thinking twice.
Devoted and caring despite the fears,
silently healing in a baptism of tears.

Tired of fighting, yet not losing hope,
viewing the fluctuating kaleidoscope.
Transforming echoes, with every turn,
floating ghosts, teach paths can burn.

Through it all, one will laugh and cry,
visions surround and teach us to fly.
Seeking kindness, memories collide,
life is awakened so take it in stride.

Error is no prison, set yourself free,
close your eyes so that you can see.
Everything contains a life in tow,
Freedom's not free…
Until you let go.

ONE NIGHT'S WINDOW

Light whispers down,
shadows animate.
Sounds becoming still,
hues detonate.
Existence streams on,
colors fluctuate.
Colored pallets wane,
portraits deviate.

Silence speaking softly,
crickets sing.
Sounds becoming visions,
minds swing.
Misty pastels dimming,
taking wing.
Calm descends quickly,
on everything.

Imagination awakened,
feeds new light.
Dark transcends swiftly,
urging twilight.

A waking gentle breeze,
just out of sight.
Creation speaking boldly,
takes a tender bite.

Stillness now exposed,
closing a blind.
Visions wildly wander,
opening a mind.
Silhouettes float images,
no depth behind.
Awakening starlit skies,
skeletons unwind.

Ashen shaded shadows,
now, just gone.
Thickened fog shifting,
new shapes drawn.
Natures gently stirring,
as life logs on.
Wakened peeking sun,
brings forth dawn.

SOUL TOUCH

An unexpected meeting

Both stop yet still you stay
transfixed not a word to say.
Heart stops and begins to pound,
time is gone, a spirit touch found.
Intense gaze into each other's soul
drawn together as a magnetic pole.
With an intense desire to delay,
you soulfully pause… and go your way.

LATER

Walk with me, do not speak,
let us wander, to that peak.
Caress the wind, smell the trees,
be Mother Earth, for this is she.
Swim the lake, touch the wood,
sense the remnant, where it stood.
Ascend this tree, reach the sky,
traverse that cloud…
Good-bye.

SOUL WARRIOR

Hard words that must be spoken,
truth is, this world's a bit broken.
A wandering, wanting your light,
out of time, then just out of sight.

Believe in truth, fight for the soul,
all that surrounds, is taking its toll.
Live life's truth, reach for its core,
releasing the spirit, till it can soar.

Make no mistakes, souls are at war,
stand till you cannot, rise any more.
We all choose, what we want to see,
it does not mean; it will come to be.

Think… Before taking flight,
forever stand, when it is right.
Courage enters the inner core,
stand and rise, a soul warrior.

MUSIC

Underneath every step a new poem,
as notes ramble to touch their tone.
Floating tunes whisper, in the fog,
as morning advances, above a bog.

Life awakens, the winds sing a song,
feathery branches, help chime along.
Into the water, the lake comes alive,
ducks and loons, freestyle their jive.

Winds wisp a chorus, into leaves,
cymbals streaming, into the trees.
Eagles flying, singing their blues,
sonatas flowing, holding the hues.

Fields glisten songs, with dew drops,
trees chant verses, from the tree tops.
Prancing fawns dance, a steady beat,
deer are wary, they stomp their feet.

Crescendos of crows, issue a squawk,
nature is stirring, as their music talks.

EYES

A walk in the woods to open my eyes,
as I gazed up, much to my surprise,
a noble bird was staring back at me.
I pause to ponder, beside a pine tree.

Our gazes locked in a respectful way,
I stood transfixed with nothing to say.
Time was still, it took my breath away,
a perpetual smile, so I decided to stay.

I spoke a whisper, it nodded its head,
as if it had heard every whisper said.
In naïve amazement our eyes talked,
gazing together as our minds walked.

In a blink of an eye, it swept the ground,
wind grazed my soul, without a sound.
I stood surveying, then let out a sigh,
with a kiss, and slow wave goodbye.

Majestic splendors put my mind on mute,
awakening eyes, with the sound of a hoot.
A magnificent owl had stopped my way,
even though it was the wrong time of day.

FIDDLEHEAD'EN

Meandering the river's shore,
gazing across the forest floor.
Pail in hand, a soothing walk,
wandering for the olive stalk.

Lifting the grass, the only trick.
discover jade; beginning to pick,
Drops in a pail, a drumming beat,
melodies stir, beneath one's feet.

Kneeling along with muddy jeans,
reaching about for emerald greens.
Pausing to stare and look about,
back in search of a little sprout.

Winds dissipate, time does pass,
colors reflect, like stained glass.
Life is alive, in the early spring,
listen as nature, begins to sing.

In silent delight, for all we see,
the best part is, the food is free.

RENEGADE

It creeps like a thief in the night,
conquering all with inner flight.
Standing alone picking up flack,
walls erected prepare for attack.

Solitary drifting leaving a stain,
creating restriction in the brain.
Fear molds and bends like clay,
sooner or later we become prey.

Expression is just a stand away,
a new sunrise, brings a new day.
Fear is no more than a disguise,
look through its glass and arise.

Wake inside where courage slept,
let vision transform in your step.
It is always near, inside us all,
now is the time to stand tall.

Fear takes hold like a renegade,
face it head on, don't be afraid.
Fear never deserves obedience,
in the heart, it makes no sense.

PALE RIDER

A rider appears upon a pale horse,
it shall seek no justice or remorse.
Gliding silently within the breeze,
spreading darkness like a disease.

The pale rider lusts for one's gold,
never let's go, once it takes hold.
Hollow words, to conceal its lies,
foggy illusions, to hide dead eyes.

A rider's treasures, fragile as glass,
rides on the wind, it will soon pass.
It has no essence, time shall reveal,
it can never learn; it can only steal.

So, stand tall for what you perceive,
reach for those who wait to believe.
Together we stand... Alone we fall,
Together united... Alone we crawl.

Hearts know a right or a wrong,
standing together forever strong.
What is right shall not ever rust,
what is wrong will turn to dust.

JULY LIGHTS

*A wandering outside on the clearest of nights,
a forest filled with mysterious flashing lights.*

    Mesmerized, what is this that I see,
    thousands of lights blinking at me.
    I run back inside, alert my friends,
    glimmering lights, that never ends!

    We run outside and freeze in awe,
    not comprehending what we saw.
    The woods now, dripping in light,
    auroras are flashing, what a sight.

    Left to right smiles, are everywhere,
    all we could do was stand and stare.
    Awakening strikes, pirouette the air,
    radiance dancing, a moment so rare.

    Seize every moment once it appears,
    firefly glows will bring you to tears.
    Seek the seconds, that nature shares,
    realize splendor, set free your cares.

    7/20/19-Ended abruptly10:12 PM

INNOCENT

Born with unconditional love.
It nurtures, gathers,
and starts to sprout.

It discovers guarded love.
It tries to flourish
yet, acquires pain.

It matures.
Realizing it can be broken,
it turns to stone.

Time crushes it into sand.
Fires of torment sear it into glass.

INNOCENCE

A door closed... I could not help...
Watching as this woman become a child.
She reached out in desperation,
touching the glass screaming.
I touched to connect with her spirit,
and felt an innocent child deep within.
Feeling the sorrow,
touching the anguish in her soul,
I had to turn away...
Again, looking back reaching for her hands,
but could not stand the pain.
Feeling her torment,
watching as she moved into the distance.
In that instant, tears blinded my eyes,
I could not turn again.
Drifting for hours...
Hoping for an opened door.

She possessed a strength I did not have.

PERSPECTIVES

A walk in the forest

My eyes sweep as they sense my crossing.
A light breeze carries an essence
of all that surrounds.
Wandering closer, I touch the evergreen.
I see its branches sweeping down,
creating shelter for all that rest beneath its limbs.

I converge to a battered birch.
There… Where it bled and mended,
teaching all, we can heal.
Here… Each mark, every curling bark,
speaks of winters conquered.

I rest upon a fallen log.
It too has its own story to tell.
Providing a home for soft green moss,
it has given life so that others survive.
Underneath a friendly chipmunk,
stops for a visit and to chat for a while.

I scan the forest… Listen.
High in a mighty pine, squirrels scurrying.
Near a brook, a partridge sits in an apple tree.
It searches for its evening meal.
It is unaware of my presence.

I gaze into the sky…
The sun is resting just above the trees,
peeking in and out creating shadows.
Imagine…Fantasies floating in air.
The sky explodes with colors.
Clouds become alive.
Dancing wildly, hues begin to soar.

Echoes of thumping wings surprises a quiet soul.
I turn my eyes to the apple tree.
A wary doe steps into the clearing.
I hold my breath… Out step two fawns.
We gaze at each other wondering and hoping.

When one sits in stillness,
life explodes right before your eyes.

VISION RISING

*In memory of my brother.
Collected thoughts of Nicholas M. Skoby Jr.*

Silent dew drops, plashing grass,
hints of sunlight, evening's glass.
A woman walks with tender feet,
upon the meadow, while I sleep.

The meadow throbs as she walks,
a gentle smile as morning talks.
Wisps of fog, enhance her glow,
why she comes; I do not know.

A lone breath moves the grass,
leaving windows, from the past.
Babbling brooks below the rain,
constant perception, of my pain.

Has she risen to bring me cheer,
as the pheasant, squirrel or deer.
Stretching out to touch her hair,
she disappeared through the air.

One lone whisper moves my lips,
as passing winds upon fingertips.
Rising wisps of her I still see,
send the maiden back for me.

FOUND POEMS

RULES OF FOUND POETRY

A "pure" *Found Poem* consists of words exclusively found in previously written text. All words must remain as they were found. Deciding which poetry form or line breaks are left to the poet. You may not change or add any words.
I chose to open a book at random and picked words from those two pages. Whatever words stood out in my mind; I wrote them down. I picked fifty to seventy-five words then crossed them out as I used them. I did not reuse words unless I had written them down more than once. These four poems were created from the book listed below.

Name of the Wind by Patrick Rothfuss
Published by Daw Books Inc.

LIT

Spark trailed a grey ash fire.
Eyes saw burst flickers
take warmth to the hands.
Sweet quiet moment
to one honest beauty,
interrupting surprised ears.
She laughed defensively.

CABARET

Composing musicians onto the stage,
sang masterwork, chorus in A.
Singing proceeded, fingers play.
Catchy design, fire, applause.
Air smell was of donkey and dust,
unwise wine and scathing innuendo.
Into the open doors.

Found poems
The Name of the Wind - Patrick Rothfuss
First poem pages 418-419 - 2nd poem page – 446
Daw books Inc

INNKEEPER

Innkeeper, empty bowls and mug here,
stew for bowls, mug missing beer.
Warm bread, more drink,
once twice thrice,
blue fire insult,
debt to be paid.
Iron, copper, and silver penny,
escape to the wind.

DEMONS

Quiet eyes watching sunlight calm.
Shadows waiting, night is walking,
creatures watching.
A dream of desire, a hungry fire,
A heart is speaking, time is tormenting,
everyone knowing,
demons.

Found poems
The Name of the Wind - Patrick Rothfuss
First poem Pages: 4-5 …2nd Pages: 172 - 173
Daw Books, Inc

INTERACTIVE POEM

*Choose any of the lines to create a poem.
Use any of these lines as the poem.
Split the lines or mix them. No Rules.*

SCRAMBLE

ravenousness rains deciding to share

suddenly the sky is hemorrhaging light

a smoldering sun commences to stream

sleepy soft scenery drifts beyond the night

whispering winds wail… This is not fair

static bursting forth as if we were not there

sounds signal silence ripping through the air

cashmere clouds censor blocking the bright

meandering rain now a rainbow dream

glistening glimpses observing the sight

waltzing nights reflection in a midnight blue

hungry hummingbirds hover just over there

as blossoms feed a cool spring breeze

savory scented florets flow to the earth

snowdrops and crocus burst with first sight

glistening grass glimmers in morning dew

fireflies ignite playing peek-a-boo

fauna franticly forages for fall foods

reaching for the spring's warm early light

fountains of greens are bathing the trees

wonder waking wishes are floating on air

springtime arrives in a glorious rebirth

meandering moose slowly and silently drift by

a waddling bear turns and stares in my direction

the fish escapes a hook, slaps my face goodbye

CREATE

CREATE

HAIKU'S

Haiku's consist of three lines
containing seventeen syllables.

*First line - five syllables.
Second line - seven syllables.
Third line – five syllables.*

RAIN
Circles on a pond
the fish and I do not care
leaves turn upside down.

INVISIBLE
The rustling leaves
alert senses to echoes
silent life exposed.

FOLIAGE
Mountain trees bursting
yellow and orange then red
autumn is itching.

LIFE
Like walking upstream
it pushes relentlessly
exactly the point.

PERSISTENCE
Insects flying by
dodging trout's every effort
success takes timing.

TWINS
Twin fawns flit the field
fluently flurrying through
footloose foolishness.

SAILING
Just float in a boat
while observing nature's note
vacant minds drifting.

FAWNS
Twin fawns on the edge
unaware of the watcher
mothers vigilant.

TIME
Today, tomorrow
the past is a procedure
change is not sorrow.

EMBRACE
Embrace what is right
so, the strong and the weary
will keep up the fight.

SILHOUETTES
The shadows in life
are now ghosts of awareness
memories of strife.

THE WOODCOCK
Out the woodcock flies
startled, straight up and away
adrenaline walks.

JOY
Rainbows in the eyes
waterfalls upon a face
overwhelmed senses.

A VOICE
Vibrations in rock
is it there or is it not?
listen to it speak.

SEED
This moment is strange
wait, I have been here before
life sight from within.

FLOAT
Time from a window
echoes of falling water
a life on a ledge.

BOTANICAL FANTASY
Hobbit's feet reaching
golden giants protruding
cobblestone walks speak.

FLOODED
Fountains reaching out
gathering childish laughter
exhaustion draws tears.

PAUSE
Distracting pathways
with stop light flashing colors
smell red, yellow, green.

GARDENS
Rock and roll plumage
scents are playing instruments
tones touch sensations.

THE FLOCK
Sentries are posted
twenty-eight marching soldiers
hens protecting pults.

GUESTS
Sushi and Saki
is the start of a party
wasabi, soy, rice.

SEAGULL
A seagull ballet
suspended on air and sea
white on a windshield.

FIREFLY
Nocturnal creatures
flashing lights in the darkness
daylight breaks the night.

CROSSROAD
Crossroads before us
left, right, forward, back, or up
fly now, straight away.

OLD TREE
Close your eyes and feel
old spirit of the hollow
acorns hit my head.

REFLECT
Try to live life soft
enveloping every part
reach the inner soul.

SURPRISE
The male pheasant runs
swaying grass moves in a wave
startled at the edge.

MYSTIFYING!
Distant stars are bright
still night, then deafening light
what the hell was that?

TIME
Too fast, too slow, wait
it has never seemed to stop
blind, it slipped away.

ROAR
The surf rises up
crashing on the horizon
screaming at the sky.

RAIN DANCE
Rhythms in the rain
wind conducts droplets on air
cumulus clouds dance.

HOUSE
A push through the brush
a fallen tree, a hollow
this is someone's home.

YOUNG FLYCATCHER
Acrobats in air
flying here and turning there
that has got to hurt!

RAINBOW
A perfect balance
between the sun and the rain
a ROY G BIV day.

BARRICADE
A beautiful coat
covered with embroidery
protecting a heart.

LESSONS
Teach me, reach me please
a singing whippoorwill speaks
life notes from above.

SHADOWS
Ricocheting light
illusions larger than life
shadowing giants.

TASTY
The maple tree bleeds
reduced to a tasty treat
transfusion complete.

DAZED
Simplicity now
translucent holes in a mind
bewildered again.

SOARING
The third eye awakes
a silver thread connecting
speed of thought reaches.

PONDER
Simplicity sparks
consciousness awakening
revelations burst.

SCURRY
A blank empty stare
an impenetrable air
stillness is not there.

MIRROR
We are just the same
I do agree we are me
we are wonderful.

KISMET
Destiny will come
twisted as the lover's knot
touch the future's call.

SPRING
Buttercup fields thrive
cloverleaf and Queen Anne's lace
life is arriving.

HEALING
A rainbow in fog
trying to reach for the sky
kindness sets it free.

CONUNDRUM
One tries to answer
the witticism with pun
neither here nor there.

CONFUSION
Scamper here and there
like breathing underwater
exactly… nowhere.

SOULLESS
Compassion fading
emptiness enters the air
hate is arriving.

LEMMINGS
We shall shadow on
exploits leading to the sea
population shift.

ALONE
No one will perceive
I'm arguing with myself
no one will hearken.

INTERSTELLAR
Nebula stirring
a spiraling galaxy
faint light circling.

E.M.P.
High speed propulsion
electro molecular
good bye control net.

SCIENCE
Matter and motion
natural philosophy
lines have been broken.

TECHNOLOGY
We are, we are not
electronics is not life
intellect losing.

KEEPING ROOM
The keeping room waits
the fireplace is ablaze
everyone hoping.

MEMORIES
Fragments of dear souls
affect memories in time
smiles begin growing.

SMILES
Sudden gusts of wind
passageways to paradise
memories float free.

RESTLESS
Inconspicuous
fully inconsiderate
sleep deprivation.

IRATE
I will tell you what
basket full of wonderful
roam your trail of tears.

THE LAST STEP
We are near the edge
soon apathy ricochets
feet caressing air.

TIDES
Do not validate
a tidal wave's cast of hate
silence will drown one.

TALK
Just a simple word
exclamation or greeting
its time has elapsed.

DOVES
A pair together
soft sounds become music
morning sonata.

SURPASS
An opaque window
surrounded clearly in thought
transcending through time.

THE RISE
Soaring in the wind
ascent accelerating
spirit advancing.

PHANTOMS
Silent faceless seas
specters move on violently
blindness is peril.

PARRY
Evading the truth
withdrawing and regrouping
lunge forward and touch.

REPEAT PARRY
Evading questions
withdrawing and regrouping
lunge forward and touch.

NOWHERE
Evading issues
you have lost and said nothing
withdraw and regroup.

HYPOCRISY
They cannot own this
they possess no intellect
but of course, I can.

THE GIFT?
A fire warms night
what! Prometheus stole it
drown it in water.

ESCALATE
Reflect carefully
it was a notable gift
send back the fire.

NOW WHAT
We have no fire
now we'll all surely suffer
pronounced idiot.

CONFER
A treasure is found
undeniably passé
speaking face to face.

DREAM
Life has clarified
energy transfers forever
everlasting dream…

LISTEN
A lesson is taught
teachers do not carry signs
an epiphany.

DAYBREAK
In through the darkness
silently slow sneaking sun
new thoughts erupting.

DAWN
Silent shadows pause
as birth ruptures the darkness
a new sight teaches.

FOX
Quickly quietly
fox flows fluidly for field
wonder, wander, wish.

BIRTH
I see the heartache
tests, trials and tribulations
and so, it begins.

DESIRE
Flagrant temptations
a soul is lost silently
searching endlessly.

PESSIMIST
I can, I cannot
no thought will be created
hopelessly gloomy.

BLAME IT ON THE PLATYPUS
They have everything
life may be an illusion
branches are not roots.

STAND
Stand up and express
indifference is naïve
be very concerned.

DAYDREAM
Seeking the rainbows
ships sail hopelessly inland
existing on hope.

TRANSPARENT
Insects and cobwebs
living life in the fast lane
light on a window.

DRIFTING
Moon meandering
the clouds silently slip by
a world turns softly.

TIME
Visions in the air
it is neither now or then
it cannot be caught.

SUNSET
Winds are soft and still
there's a levitating moon
aura clouds ramble.

THOUGHT 1
Liquid thoughts drifting
the ballpoint ignoring flow
imagery verse drifts.

MYSTIC
Astral connection
a perplexing mystery
spirit is flowing.

CARITAS
Divisions must stop
realize together now
love is meant for all.

THINK
Life will be the muse
inspirations will follow
meditate in thought.

THE ARTIST
A vocal pallet
choosing words so carefully
painting apathy.

THE WEB
Web on a window
meticulously woven
morning dew glitters.

SPIDER
Hidden near its' trap
set to catch the evening lights
skilled opportunist.

GHOSTS
Unperceivable
stretching slowly as it sets
shadows from the sun.

WINDTALKERS
Winds speak in whispers
a stillness in the meadows
softly comes the flight.

NATURE
Imposing grandeur
complete beauty encompassed
majestic splendor.

NOCTURNAL
Life auras appear
throughout the dark atmosphere
success emerging.

DISTRACTED
Drawn into the light
as stillness is compromised
blinded silently.

THOUGHT 2
Surrounded by locks
teaching all that it touches
no keys set one free.

VISION
A walk-through darkness
just a single star in sight
blind creatures follow.

BULLYING
Sharp cutting signals
piercing beyond heart and mind
Kevlar cannot shield.

THE LEDGE
Shame is distorted
an edge has been crossed over
compassion falling.

THE BRINK
Hopeless meander
bleakly seeking nirvana
a world is breaking.

THE WEIGHT
Carefully engage
you will live what you harvest
life in a balance.

RISE
Angry rhetoric
disconnected compassion
reach beyond, be still.

A REASON
A seed is planted
blizzards and tormented clouds
life still emerges.

FRIENDS
Hues in a rainbow
rays of sunshine in the clouds
lights ignite darkness.

EQUINOX
The geese are talking
colors dressing for the show
autumn exploding.

FOOTPRINT
Walk lightly through time
save inspirations for all
shadows on a page.

LIVE
Seeking adventure
pursuing a golden fleece
chasing does not touch.

UNBREAKABLE
There is simple truth
there is an everlasting
incorruptible.

SPARK
Pure simplicity
inspirations emerge fourth
it is not the thought.

SEEKING HAPPINESS
A bordered frontier
with accomplished instruction
exploding the edge.

THE WALK
A downward incline
an upward summit are twins
elevations rise.

REALIZE
Lost in a moment
subconsciously daydreaming
an awakening.

GREED
Children are falling
surrounded by ignorance
blood in the water.

FREEZE
Shocking images
imbedded into the mind
immobile in time.

NIGHTSKY
Scintillating lights
silhouetted figures freeze
vastness shaded blue.

THOUGHT 3
Engage intellect
a wondrous wonderland
methodical minds.

CONNECTED
River flows gently
life erupts from its shoreline
sense its connection.

THE SONG
Dewdrops floating down
each droplet a varied tone
igniting music.

SMILE TOO
I heard a whisper
wandering through the forest
smiles are everywhere.

EMERGING
An awakening
happening in a moment
hope remains alive.

EXCITEMENT
Blood pumping faster
adrenaline is flowing
realize adventure.

WHISPERS
Floating between time
walking through life silently
listen, nature speaks.

ICY
Each step with caution
freezing communication
life becomes silent.

HUNGER
Famine of the minds
not feeding in paradise
starving for freedom.

BRIGHT
Realizing courage
is a castle in the clouds
finding its freedom.

STAGES
Everyone's been lost
everything is similar
welcoming of life.

WISDOM
Let it run its course
there is nothing we can do
awaken logic.

DURABLE
Never give up dreams
truth will always find a way
hope is arriving.

KALEIDOSCOPE
Watch the shards unite
they are fragments of a whole
united with color.

APPLE TREES
Fragrant aromas,
treetops exploding blossoms
life does find its way.

CREATE

THOUGHTS

TIME

An auburn leaf is lifted over the snow
by a chilly breeze in mid-winter…
It begins to realize its journey has not yet ended.

As each individual snowflake drifts in air,
it will rest as one.

The caterpillar does not perish,
it bursts forth with wings.

If you see a tear fall from an angel's eye,
there will be no need for words.

There are some that have passed
that look over me.
I swear I hear their laughter from heaven.

Time is an excellent therapy;
let time find you.
Introduce yourself.

If one squanders away the seconds,
one will never discover its moments.
Time should not have a clock.

Time cannot be bought and sold,
but it can and will cost you.

Time...
Now is its essence.

We all have restraints, sorrows and regrets.
There is no justice in this prison,
time becomes still.

What is the importance of time?
Is it the footprints of what one leaves behind?

If time reveals truth, can truth be touched?

Time will not travel to a direct result.

We seem to be surrounded by time.
No time to contemplate, no time to dream,
no time to reflect.

The only footsteps of substance
are the strides one is taking right now.

One will never understand yesterday
or tomorrow… Without today.

If we do not release the past,
we shall never grasp today.

One cannot change what is,
by wishing what is not.

I was not.
Only to find out I was.
But… I was not.

Time is limitless,
However,
Time is not what matters.

Time offers us many diverse interests.
A path may lead in many directions.
Live life forward and eventually
you will touch what is meant to be.

It never matters how many do not accept
you for who you are,
when you find those that do.

Practice becomes the teacher.

When one journeys to seek life,
one will surely find their own.

I dislike getting up early to an alarm clock going off. I dislike early or late telephone calls because my first thoughts are that something is or has gone wrong. I dislike getting up early to look out a window in the winter and not being able to see out. I guess I do not like getting up early.

  Must be my point of view.

I love waking up early to an alarm clock to spend a day fishing. I love rising to early telephone calls to talk with family or friends. I love getting up early to look out a window to see all the wildlife greet the new day. I guess I love waking up early.

  Is it just a point of view?
Life is full of contradictions.

SILENCE

Silence can speak.
Your silence taught me
that I had failed.

Some moments scream for silence.
Silence is an achievement.

Silence provides a mirror
that can reflect tranquility.

Silence is deafening
as it reaches
to awaken.

Silence becomes stillness.

We have two eyes,
two ears,
two nostrils
and one mouth.
So, should we
look, listen and breathe,
twice as much as we speak?

But, wait… What about the brain?
There are four parts to the brain.
Should we use the brain twice as much as
the eyes, ears and nostrils and
four times as much as one's mouth?

There should be more silence.

Memories heal.
They ride the whispers in the wind,
and the smiles in one's heart.
Traverse these winds.

Kindness cannot be possessed.
It must be given.

When you fall,
the number of people that are there to catch you,
may define your life.

Darkness fails when silence rises.
Silence falls when darkness rises.
Stillness resists when evil rises.
Evil fails when stillness rises.

In a battle between the mind and the spirit,
trust the spirit.

Can the mind overwhelm the spirit?

Silence can and will speak.

Wisdom contains smiles.
Smiles contain silence.

Silence contains wisdom.
All senses are awakened.

Love can be
a feather in the wind,
or the dandelion seed.
Lifting one up;
floating freed.

What starts a smile?

It is challenging to seek simplicity,
Even though it surrounds us.

The thought is but a wish,
the dream reaches achievement.

A decision right or wrong is still correct.
Indecision is rooted in fear.

The greatest wealth is silent.
The ultimate treasure is the light
that is right in front of you.

There can be no knowledge
without imagination.

I have yielded my life to chance. I cannot account for its patterns, nor the causes or effects. Fate has thrust me forward into opportunities that I might have never comprehended if I was in control. My path meanders. My lessons are infinite. With every step I have discovered a new
        and exciting fragment of life.

Fragments of life are learned as we traverse the physical world. To truly understand life, one must traverse their spirit. Then we can weave through the dimensions of time and space and travel at the speed of thought.
    The spirit floats free…In a silent relaxed mind.
        Worlds await.

        If not today…
        When?

LIFE

Life is as the spring river,
flowing wild and free.
It can sweep one by swiftly, or
deliver one to a gentle serene pool.

Life is simple.
Learning this can be intense.

Life is an adventure,
that is meant to be shared.

Life is larger than one yet,
should be lived as one.

Someone yelled out, "Heads up!"
I looked up...
Got smacked in the face with reality!

Life is not a one-way street,
unless, we were meant to travel
the wrong way through it.

Every step is a beginning,
every step is an end.
The path has not perished... It has grown.

Your travels will never approach
their vanishing point.

Every step reveals a new perspective.

A friend said to my son, "I feel bad for deaf people who watch the news, because they are not getting the full story." My son turned back to him and said, "Then we are all deaf."
I smiled.
Life lessons and smiles are everywhere.

When one is surrounded by murky waters,
the best solution is to be still.

Life never travels to a direct result.
If one avoids life,
it will still approach.

Death interrupts,
it does not yield,
it does not carry a sign.

Brown would be yellow,
red would be green,
grey would be blue if they could.
What would you be?

If you do not recognize obstacles in life,
will you become one?

Persistence always
defeats failure and disappointment.
Dedication should be stubborn.

On an avenue of pain and screams,
clawing, grabbing at your dreams,
what lies before is not as it seems,
Smoky mirrors are their schemes.
Never drink from their tainted cup.
Never give in... Never give up!

Change, like time, is inevitable.
One may not perceive either,
but with or without you it will occur.

One is either part of a solution,
or part of a problem.
Life seeks simplicity.

A square peg can fit into a round hole!

One can see and smell smoke.
One can see and feel fire.
One cannot stop either,
unless one searches,
finds and destroys
the spark.

There is a stillness in the night.
Let the ears and mind take flight.
One will soon find an inner light.
Resolve will reveal another sight.

What begins and ends life?

The mind is an access to the soul,
silence is the entrance to infinity.

Love and hate are twins.
Life and death are twins.
They evolve from the same parents.

Each breath one takes offers a key to life.
It clears the mind, boosts energy, gives warmth,
enhances touch, sight, speech, smell and sound.
Ignore distractions.

Truth has a trap door.
One must possess courage to lift and uncover it.

One may create missteps in life, but
with every misstep one becomes wiser.

When you reach for truth
be sure all senses are alert.
Answers may lie within.

Being clever is not wisdom.
Knowledge is not intelligence.
Wisdom is not intelligence nor knowledge.
Clever.

I am not the person I was.
I am not the person I want to be.
I am not the person I could be.
I am not the person I will be.
I am…

When souls connect,
trust the soul.

There are always trials and tribulations in life. One must reflect to travel past them. Some paths one will walk alone. Other paths will lead one to intersect and relate with others. Some of these meetings there will be no true interaction, while others may help one to learn, laugh, love, cry, or feel anger. Seek all crossroads in life, with patience, compassion and perception.
In a brief moment...
Some may touch for a lifetime!

Many lines of pure intention have been crossed. One must discover how to recognize these thoughtless intentions. What should be tolerated, what should not. When lines of pure intention have been betrayed, one must consider when to stand and when to withdraw. Have you discovered when to stand and when to retreat?

Life can be as quicksand.
The more one struggles,
the deeper it draws one in.

Life can be as delicate as the pine branch.
It can bend, accepting a climb,
or it can snap from its burden.

The highest tides
can cleanse many misjudgments.
It cannot purify all of them.

Life is all encompassing.
Troubled life leads to troubled lives.

Conflicts make a soul hurt.

My truth, your truth.
Your pain, our pain.
Everything and everyone's world.

The less one wants and needs,
one comes closer to freedom.

As clouds conceal the sun or moon,
a world turns and winds gust,
to clear one's views.

Wander the lives that have passed…
Wonder… Were they proud of what they left.
Wish… We will leave as much as they have.

When one chooses what surrounds them,
it will define them.
When one does not choose…
Do not allow what surrounds to define.

Life is a gift.
Feel, listen, smell, taste, breath and perceive.

There is relentlessly another road.
It lies just in front of you.
Take that step.

One has to feel life,
for it to touch.
Life will touch,
before one can perceive.

Life is always here,
flowing beyond every surface.
Sense everything.

I was walking through the woods,
turned to look… Déjà vu!

Fishing is never about the fish.
It is about the memories shared
by friends and family that have
caught those moments
while fishing.

Experiences come and go,
but friends are forever.

Definitions cannot define success.
Only you can.

Imagination is the strength
that can burst every lock.
It will always defeat failure.
Failure is never permanent.

Life invades without consent
as it delivers its teachings.
Eventually it becomes life absorbed.

There are no wrong answers,
for those who have thought about the question.

Life is a clarification of an everlasting dream.

FEAR

If one lives in fear,
one will become part of it.

Never let fear change what is right.
Greed and control do not contain tolerance.
They know persistence too well.
They will cross lines that should not be crossed.
Smile, because within every line is an edge.
In time, their feet will caress air.

Fear stops kindness.
Mistrust stops kindness.
Cruel encounters stop kindness.
Kindness stops fear.
Kindness stops mistrust.
Kindness may not stop cruel encounters,
but it may stop and prevent loneliness.

Proportions have many dimensions.
Do not blow them up.
One will surely plummet.

When anything takes more than it has provided,
it will eventually become surpassed.

Fear blinds what is absolute and free.
Fear passes control to others.
It soon becomes domination.

Fear destroys from the inside.
It keeps one from being themselves.
It takes courage to defeat it.

Fear demands one's obedience.
Love will never ask.

TEACHERS

So many tired, so many lost,
so many fallen.
Can the few inspire?

I endeavor to challenge myself
with thoughts of another.
Teachers are everywhere.

Teachers are born from a thought.

If one does not seek courage,
one cannot discover it.

When one has an epiphany,
we never see it coming.

Truth shall eventually find the searching mind.

Truth has many disguises.
A surface does not reveal its roots.
When searching for truth,
it usually comes down to all.

One should always listen.
The gift is what one will perceive.

Wisdom does not always realize itself…
It just is.

Lessons are never over until all life that teaches
or the minds that search and question…
Expire.

I stood in the sand as the ocean waved to me.
Its beauty beckoned me to come closer.
As I stood at the water's edge;
a wave knocked me down
and tried to pull me out.
It had not been waving to me.

I have learned from navigating life.
Teachers are everywhere,
they do not wear signs.

One can give up on life.
Life will never give up on you.

Life is not a stage.
It is a nucleus.

From the first day a child is born it begins to absorb. A child opens its eyes and collects data. The child becomes a computer, seizing all knowledge from its domain.
    Be mindful what a child will download!

The web...
The net...
No wonder it traps you!

An incomplete thought
is an unfinished thought.
It usually transforms into hours of thought.

If not for the questions,
there can be no solutions.

Inside every question lies an answer.
A point of view is not the answer.
The first answer may not be the final answer.

The importance of knowledge
is what one will do with it.

A cruel temperament is similar
to spring rivers…
Swollen, wild and reckless.
A soft temperament is similar
to the sheltered pond…
Quiet, serene and still.

If you were transparent
would you perceive yourself?
Could one touch you?
Would you look through yourself?

Fledgling birds fly alone
in search of a yearning.
They do not query; they soar head on.

Hate rarely carries a sign.

There are many reasons
not to stop and help someone in need.
There is only one reason to do it.

A total stranger tries to comfort you.
Why would they do that?
How did they know?

If I wanted friends that agree with me,
I would buy a mirror.

The further one drifts,
the closer one gets to life.
The closer one gets to life,
the more one wants to float.

When discussing different points of view
without anger, the outcome does not matter.
All learn... All grow.

Which is more important?
Intellect or experience.
Intellect thinks, experience does.
They are the ultimate team.
They should surely be partners.

Which is more important?
Past, present, or future.

The beauty of a lady slipper
hides its fragile nature.
Its roots are long and shallow,
they must not be distressed to flourish.

Sunflower stalks reach high to reach for the sun.
Its flower is large to accent its beauty,
its abundant harvest nurtures.

To truly grow,
be as the apple tree.
May your branches reach light,
and your roots become strong.
Endure, bud and blossom.
Feed, live, and feel all that you reach…
You will bear fruit.

Animals have a way
of drawing out your soul.
Animals do not critique.
Friendships are unconditional.

At times, animals
and humans are one.

If one does not see themselves,
they will not perceive others.

I have never stood alone, or rejected silence.
I never needed anything that I did not have.
I have fallen and gotten back up.
Someone or something
has always reached and taught me.

When seeking to learn something,
be sure you understand it.
It will be there for life.
When you do not understand something
be sure you realize that.
It may save your life!

I was surrounded by your thoughts.
Now what?
Should I surrender?

The lone wolf is never alone.

Deceit will not remain,
it is the rigid tree.
Truth is the autumn leaf,
yielding, strong and freed.

Every thought and every experience
changes one's essence.

Nature holds a natural, everlasting truth.
Its visions are not fragmented.
It is not infinite.

Stand in a place where your ancestors stood.
Reminisce in their childhood.
Would you live there?

Fishing is the call of a loon,
reflections of the moon,
winds on the water,
rain on your face,
calm in a cove,
stillness,
smiles,
laughs,
but most of all… Time.

I have known people who
were right all the time.
They never understood the question.

Why am I here?
Why are they here?

When one forgives, journeys carry no burdens.

When in need of answers,
they will be all around.
Watch... Sense...
Before they smack you in the face!

When one has a problem,
do not search for answers from others.
Examine points of view and thoughts,
but the only true answer lies in you.

When one discovers someone
with nothing to give...
Listen very carefully!

Nature can take one to the edge,
then... Teach you to let go.

STRENGTH

There is a profound majesty in the lion,
its heart is strong and intense.

The tiger is a fierce solitary hunter,
its hunger is its strength.

The solitary wolf is ferocious,
yet, its power lies within a pack.

In nature, there are predators and prey.
Sometimes the prey escapes.
The strongest survive.
Be aware… Beware…
Be still…

Our strength has always been in unity.

To forgive someone takes time.
The longest winding journey,
is the one to forgive oneself.

I once met a person I thought had no wall. As I approached, I walked right into their wall. It was fragile and transparent. I hoped it would not shatter. I took great care to respect the life before me. I reached out my hand to touch this life.

They looked right through me.

I believe in you.
I will pick you up when you fall.
I will be your support,
when you lose strength.
When you are wounded,
I will help you heal.
I believe in you...
You must believe in yourself!

Respectful conversations lead to knowledge;
even when points of view differ.

Do not chase a dream, it will misuse time.
Dare to dream, worlds awaken.

A dream can endlessly be reached.
If one's dream fails, do not alter the dream,
adjust one's path to it.

If every step one takes is never rejected,
why not take a journey?

Destiny will always be personal.

SENSES

There is no sight for the hopelessly lost.
There is no scent for a burning wish.
There are no sounds to a broken heart.
There is no touch to damaged trust.
There is no savor to a bitter mind.
There are no words for a beaten soul.

There is a touch for the hopelessly lost.
There is an echo for a burning wish.
There are lyrics for a broken heart.
There is a hint for damaged trust.
There is a taste to the bitter mind.
There are visions for a beaten soul.

In stillness you can always discover.
See, taste, smell, listen, and touch.
Insight will burst forth.

COURAGE

It cannot be spoken,
it cannot be taken.
It does not have to be realized
for one to possess it.
It is not a thought,
it is never wrong.
It is, or it is not.
It is a silent action,
with a loving soul.

Danger does not carry a sign,
courage understands that.

Be a voice for those who are afraid to speak.
Motivate those who have not reached.
Teach those that do not understand.

FAILURE

Failure is part of life,
accept and move on.

Own failures.
It clarifies strength.

If one never fails,
one has not tried.
Perseverance will always defeat failure.

One is never done with failure.
It remains a few steps ahead,
and a few steps behind.
Failures encompass life.

Failures are life lessons that teach.
Keep trying, one is not there yet,
but one is getting closer.

Smile... Laugh!

LOVE

Love cannot be possessed
but it can be held.

Love cannot be grasped,
but it can touch.

Love can be invisible,
but it never leaves.

Love can hurt…
Is that the beauty of it?

Love can be as complex as silence,
or as simple and humble as… "How are you?"

As a bead of water clings to the window pane,
the sun will ignite its rainbow.

WINTER

Winter's trees teach us,
it is about life within.

Winter's life is not dormant,
it is reflective.

A soft coating of snow reminds me,
we all need a hug now and then.

When one loses everything,
what does one gain?

If I had hindsight,
I would not know
if I was coming or going.

PARADISE

If fenced in a world with only one gateway out into a larger, beautiful universe; would you try to learn a way through that gate? With every step, there would be consequences and rewards that slow you down. The harder the fight, the more the obstructions keep the gate out of reach. Some will try to stop you. Will you stop trying because it is in your nature to do so? Will you keep trying to reach the goal? Are you happy in your world, and will you remain there? Will you walk the fence line trying to find the gate; missing all the life inside? Will you accept what lies before you? It seems so many choices lay before us, but do we see them?
In time, life transcends this gate. No obstructions,
      no consequences and no more ordeals.
    Relax... Life is worth the journey!

THE MIND

The mind is a wonderful instrument. Dedication and practice allow it to travel time and create worlds of marvel and imagination. The mind can express emotion, process pain, touch ecstasy, and tears. It allows us to realize beauty, connect with nature and explore the heavens. It tastes foods, smells the rain, hears a bird's song, observes a sunset, and understands the winds touch. The mind can sense everything.
Remember...
an instrument must be rehearsed
to reveal beautiful music.

Knowledge, Decency, Ground and Sense...
What has happened to common?

Common is no longer common.
It is used less...Not useless.

P

Puppets peered past portals perhaps proving parachuting porcupines probably pinned Partridge's pierced plumage. Puffins plugged pebbles past penguins pushing pouting pedigree poodle's past political points. Proving procrastinating politicians, probably poppycock!

T

Tail the Toad took Time the Tapir to Tig the Tiger's. They traveled to Two-thirty Towhee's to talk to Tina Toucan. Terence the Tanager, then traversed to Tough Tin Tuna's to telephone Tom Tom Turkey's teepee. Taking tambourines, tomahawks, trumpets, trombones too; truly traveling troubadours. They traveled to Tom Tom's, there Ted told Tabitha, two tabbies, to teach Time the Tapir to travel through the tunnel to the trestle, then to the tavern to taste the theater's tea. Terrific!
                    Then ten together.
                Terribly, troubling theater.

IMAGINE

What if most of what you were taught
was not true?

Are there more than two sides to every story
because we live in a three-dimensional world?

If you were a single atom,
what would the world around you look like?

Can magnetic fields that surround us
produce energy?

Is it possible to leave your body consciously?

Can a truth be a lie?

Can colors heal?

What is your meaning of Life?

MEMORIES

Memories are the tears in one's eyes
and the smiles on one's face.

Memories are not about what one has lost,
but what one has found.
What have they found in you?

There can be no growth
without memories.

Memories cannot exist
without being touched.

Memories are adventures,
for those that have touched.
What will your next one be?

Memories touch one's most profound moments.

THE TOUCH

Touch me.

The reach…
the touch...
silence together.

Touch me.

She spoke of life, of love and lies,
the give and take, the compromise.
Tones of truth, words of the wise,
as freedom spoke, to cut her ties.
She trusted me.

WHY

Why can words pierce a soul,
when one cannot touch them?
Can you feel a word's soul?

Why do stars stay where they are?
Is there no wind in space?
Can they float; are they weightless?

Why does not grange and orange rhyme?
Should it be spelled ohrange?

Why is bass a fish when it can be a guitar,
singer or a sound. Isn't that a little fishy?

"Why," is every question.
"Because," is every answer.
"Why," questions life.
"Because," lives life.
Together they are life.

Wander... Wonder... Wish...

THE MARIONETTES

Their world exists on a small stage safe from the troubles and worries of the rest of world. They were stored in a small box for travels, strings nicely groomed and straightened before each show. People highly anticipated the acclaimed performances. Soon it would be show time. The crowds rushed to their seats in anticipation of the marionette show. The curtains opened and all stared as the puppets sang and danced on the small stage. People were mesmerized as they laughed and cheered the performance. They hardly noticed the strings anymore, until near the end of the show, out walked a puppet with no strings. It was not made of wood but of a soft plastic. No one was sure what to make of it until the marionettes started to throw wooden letters at the plastic puppet. A's, I's, R's, S's and X's flew through the air just bouncing off the puppet, until the wooden marionettes picked him up and threw him off their stage. Some people cheered some were appalled, yet all were entertained. Not one questioned who controlled the marionette's strings.

CREATE

CREATE

CREATE

JUST FOR FUN

PICTURE THESE

Hang a dartboard
on the back of a closed door.

Use a can of shaving cream
as a hammer.

Take a friend outside in the dark to show them
the deep hole that you dug in your backyard.

Leave an iron rake on the ground with its
tines up, especially when you are trying
to teach your child why not to do it.

Call a Great Dane while he is sleeping
under a table.

Stand close to anyone telling you they can get the camp fire started in the rain, while they are holding a can of gasoline.

Cook pasta without water,
because they advertise it
as waterless cookware.

Assume that if someone else has done it
you can too.

Spread black mulch throughout your
yard when you have a white pet.

I had nothing to do so,
I had to do something.

Today is tomorrow,
yesterday was today.

Picture a person in a canoe towing a stalled
speed boat to a landing.
As in life, it is not the speed that counts,
it is all about getting there.

Never say never.
It is too lingering.

My bucket list:
Blueberries
Eggs
Apples
Tomatoes
Chicken

When I was young, I loved to climb trees.
Now I hug them to hold myself up,
so that my crunchy bones don't break.

I guess I let the cat out of the bag.
It's not my fault,
who the hell put it in there?

Take the bull by the horns.
Now what?

Turn over a new leaf.
So… I ripped off a leaf
turned it upside down.
Now what?

What exactly is a thingamajig?
A dance, a fishing lure?
Is it related to a thingamabob?

Is thingy an abbreviation?
Are doodads the same as doohickeys?
Is a gizmo a whatzits or a widget?
Jumping Jehoshaphat!

Am I supposed to count forty winks?

How miniscule are the
wee small hours of the night?
It is exhausting searching for them.

If attention spans get any shorter,
I would already be exhausted.

If you don't get it,
commit yourself.

I am at a loss for words.
Now what?

THRILL OF A LIFETIME

"Hey, Skoby, you're crazy. Look what I just found! Lake Placid, New York is now allowing the public to ride the half mile bobsled run, and full luge runs. That should get your adrenaline pumping!" So, it began… A new adventure that started the thrill of a lifetime.

A few weeks later we were there. After signing three waivers, I stood on one of the bridges over the bobsled track. I noticed this was nothing like on television, the speeds were incredible! The last quarter mile was straight up hill and they barely stopped before hitting the wall and that was only the half mile run. I began to feel a profound sense of impending doom… But I was all in!

I was the number two man in the sled with a professional driver in front and a professional brake man in the back, my friend was in the third spot. Once we were in the sled, we got these brief instructions: Do not hit the driver in the back with any part of your body and do not tilt your head out for a better look. We were off, the first thing I did on the first turn was hit the driver in the back with my head, as I fought to push myself off him my head tilted to the right and bounced off the wall snapping my head to the left. I was now in survival mode, I thought to myself, just hold on and stay straight up. By this time, I could see the wall, it was over. When I got out of the sled, I checked my body parts, all was good but, I didn't remember much of the ride. When I took off my gloves, I notice my knuckles were still white. I pondered for about an hour with my adrenaline pumping and I began to theorize that I had already done the two worst things. How much worst could it get? Back I went for two more runs but still hit the driver with my head.

The next adventure was the luge. The first time down I slowly pushed myself off and had a leisurely ride down. It had its moments but, after the bobsled, the speed felt a little too slow. So, the next time I had the person at the top give me a good push and I pushed as fast as I could with my hands. Oh, yeah, the speed was there! I was out of control just about from the start. No matter how many times I tried to right myself it did not help. I felt myself ricocheting off one wall to the next all the way down, thank goodness for helmets! A few times I thought I was going to come flying out of the track. At the bottom, I took a few moments to try to recover, ok, maybe I misspoke. Minutes! It was more like minutes! I felt like I had fallen down a mountain hitting every rock on the way down. That was to be the last of my luge runs. As for the bobsled runs. There would always be next year.

YEAR TWO

Off we went to Lake Placid to bobsled again. As soon as we hit the bobsled track, we were in for a big surprise. They now offered, for those who dared, a run on the full mile track. It was a chance of a lifetime. My friend and I were all in. We kept the same positions however; the directions were just a little different. Do not hit the driver in the back, because he could lose control and flip the sled. They couldn't have said that just a tad earlier, like when we were not in the sled. Of course, the part about, do not tilt your head to the left or right, I learned that one already so, I thought. Now for the new one, you will be experiencing about three G's of force on the turn called Shady, keep your arms stiff and push back with all your force or your head will be forced down between your knees. Laughing inside, I felt perfectly comfortable because I knew I was not capable of putting my head between my knees. Apparently, I had no idea of the power of G force, nor did I understand fully what was about to happen. Ignorance is bliss, no matter how brief.

We sat in the sled as the driver and brakeman pushed us off. We hit Shady at about ninety miles an hour. G force should have been called brute force. The joke was on me. There I was with my head not only between my knees but, I was kissing the sled. *Just a reminder, I cannot physically do that!* The rest of the ride I struggled to right myself up and finally accomplished this feat on the last straight away. Talk about adrenaline. I saw relief coming as I saw the last quarter mile that was straight up hill. *Just a note, the last quarter mile is excluded from the mile run, because you are already past the finish line.* Upon exiting the sled, the idiot inside me jumped up and said, "Hey, can we go again?" The driver took off his helmet and said laughingly "Are you guys out of your minds? You are the first people to ever say that." We were totally serious because we could not feel the pain with all the adrenaline flowing. He said "Sure, let's go." We took two more rides and the driver and brakeman must have thought we were capable, or crazy. I invited them for drinks but the driver said he was allergic to alcohol, I asked him how did you ever get to be allergic to alcohol? He laughed and said, "every time I have a drink, I break out in handcuffs." As we parted, they asked us to come back early the next day.

The second day we had about the same results until the last run. Everything seemed to fall in place. We were enjoying rides without the panic. I remember nothing about the runs except they were the thrill of my life. So, once again they invited us back for a *"real"* ride. We had no idea what that meant, but we were all in.

The next morning, we took three rides. We helped push the sled and then jump in. I was starting to notice my surroundings and I actually began to feel the track beneath me. I fought the G force and finally kept my body up. Life was good. Just a slight head bump against the wall for a second of two, no big deal until I took off my helmet and saw the damage. We headed up to the bobsledder's hut to get me a new helmet. Inside the hut were seasoned bobsledders, one of them asked if we were bobsledders. I said, "We are learning." One of them saw my helmet and said, "hey that is not damage; let me show you damage". Out from his locker he pulled out a helmet that was at least one third gone. Then they all started pulling out helmets. The worst was literally split in half. Then someone asked if we had crashed yet? "No," I answered, *thinking, thanks for putting that thought in my head*! "I guess you're not bobsledders yet," they all said. We shook hands and headed for our fourth ride.

From the start, we knew there was something different. We did not know what, it was; just a feeling. We ran, pushed and jumped in. I didn't hit the driver in the back. When we hit Shady my head was up and my arms where straight and I could feel the track beneath me. I could see the turns ahead of time and leaned into each turn. Most importantly my head did not hit the wall. I was relaxed and enjoying the ride. When we reached the bottom, the driver jumped out of the sled and turned toward the time shack. The time shack door flew open and the man was shaking his head. We had no idea what that was about. Luckily, family and friends were videotaping the entire day. We asked if we could go again, they laughed and commented even professionals are only allowed four rides a day. Sadly, we headed to the hotel room. We decided to eat and watch the video of our day. Someone noticed that the world record for the track seemed very close to our time. We ran it back and wrote down the record time and froze the video on our time.

Our time was 60.01 the track and Olympic record was 59.75. Then all the pieces fell into place, we began to understand what we had accomplished. Not bad for a couple of rookies. We all decided to hit the town and have dinner and a drink or two. We were so excited about what we had done we started to brag a little more.

We came to one of the shops on Main street where a gentleman was outside and overheard us bragging. He stopped us and said "did you really come close to the world record on the bobsled run?" Yes, we did we all piped in. He said "I'm going to do you a favor, I'm on the Olympic committee, how would you boys like to join the Olympic team?" My immediate reaction was to burst out into laughter and I said as I unzipped my coat, "Hey, look at me, I'm a sausage. Can you imagine what I'd look like in one of those suits. I'm a lot older than you think." He got very serious and said "hey, you know how old the man was that won the gold medal in Japan for bobsledding?" Yes, I said, he was in his mid-forties. Not saying a word about being past that. He continued and said, "I am writing this number down and when you get home call the number. They will tell you all you need to know about joining the Olympic team." Of course, we thought it was a joke, but I put the number in my pocket walking away feeling inflated and flattered. We enjoyed the rest of our day dog sledding and snowmobiling; then left for home.

 I thought about calling but my friend and I still thought it was a joke. Two weeks went by and I decided to call, just to see who would answer. To my surprise it was the Olympic Committee. I briefly told them my story and they said the first step was to get a physical from my doctor saying I was healthy and able. I panicked; no way was a doctor going to let me do it at my age. So, I called and got an appointment anyway. I told my friend the number was legitimate but he declined to follow through.

 My appointment at the doctors was brief. I gave him the form that he had to fill out and sign. He read it and looked up at me smiling. I jumped right up and said, "this is no joke. This is my one in a million shot. Check everything, but no matter what you find, do not take this from me. Please, fill out the form and give it back to me to send to the Olympic Committee." Not a word was spoken while he poked and checked me. He was smiling the entire time. He finally signed and handed me the form. Thinking I was just given my golden ticket, I thanked him and left. Two or three weeks later I got a letter stating that I was now a member of the Olympic team. The entire time thinking they must be really short of people crazy enough to fly down an ice track at about ninety miles an hour and then get back in and do it again.

My next step was to show up for an entire week the next February, for the New York games. The winning sled automatically receives the honor of going to the games for the upcoming winter Olympics.

To make a long story short I never did make it to the games, but I will always think of the two men that had allowed me this journey and the real bobsledders that accepted me for who I was. It did not bother me that I could not be there, the thoughts and thrills will always remain. Nothing can take away those years and the thrill of my lifetime!

If one has a sense for adventure, go with it.
One will never know what doors will open,
until you try.

I often wonder what my next exploration will be.

*Life will never be perfect,
but, in the end,
it will all make perfect sense.*

Thank You

Lightning Source UK Ltd.
Milton Keynes UK
UKHW012242170120
357183UK00002B/5/J